motherhood

MATTERS

motherhood

MATTERS

JOYFUL REMINDERS *of the*
DIVINITY, REALITY, *and*
REWARDS *of*
MOTHERHOOD

CONNIE E. SOKOL

CFI
An Imprint of Cedar Fort, Inc.
Springville, Utah

ISBN 13: 978-1-4621-1018-6

Published by CFI, an imprint of Cedar Fort, Inc., 2373 W. 700 S., Springville, UT 84663
Distributed by Cedar Fort, Inc., www.cedarfort.com

LIBRARY OF CONGRESS CATALOGING-IN-PUBLICATION DATA

Sokol, Connie E., author.
  Motherhood matters : joyful reminders of the divinity, reality, and
rewards of motherhood / Connie E. Sokol.
      pages cm
  Summary: Delivers practical, substantial insights that moms can really use
in daily life, while offering much-needed time away. Includes ideas to help
with de-stressing, testimony building, protecting the family, teaching life
skills, finding joy in motherhood, patience, love, setting appropriate
boundaries, and finding joy in homemaking.
  ISBN 978-1-4621-1018-6
  1. Motherhood--Religious aspects--Church of Jesus Christ of Latter-day
Saints. 2. Parenting--Religious aspects--Church of Jesus Christ of
Latter-day Saints. I. Title.

  BX8641.S639 2012
  248.8'431--dc23

                              2011046323

Cover design by Angela D. Olsen
Cover design © 2012 by Lyle Mortimer
Edited and typeset by Kelley Konzak

Printed in the United States of America

10 9 8 7 6 5 4 3 2 1

Printed on acid-free paper

To my fabulous family for giving me the gift of being a mother, and for daily helping me learn and treasure what motherhood truly means.

Praise for *Motherhood Matters*

"With years of experience, extensive research, and a twist of good humor, Connie Sokol has captured the essence and importance of motherhood with delightful stories and inspiring wisdom."

—RICHARD AND LINDA EYRE
NEW YORK TIMES BESTSELLING AUTHORS OF
TEACHING YOUR CHILDREN VALUES

"What a compelling and inspiring little book! It lifts and confirms that motherhood is a divine calling from God, the heartbeat that keeps the world on track. This is a book that should be read by every mother and grandmother."

—GARY AND JOY LUNDBERG
AUTHORS OF *I DON'T HAVE TO MAKE EVERYTHING ALL BETTER*

"We love this book! It's inspirational, practical, and humorous. To use the popular vernacular, 'It is a good read!' I'm looking forward to buying one for each of my daughters for Mother's Day or any day."

—DOUG AND GERI BRINLEY
AUTHORS AND SPEAKERS

Contents

The Divinity of Motherhood

The Reality of Motherhood

The Rewards of Motherhood

Acknowledgments

Writing this book while pregnant with my seventh child has been unbelievably timely. My overwhelming gratitude goes to my Heavenly Father, who perfectly orchestrated this spiritually deepening opportunity and helped the words flow despite the times I was in the throes of morning sickness.

To my amazing family, whom I so bone-deep adore. Thanks for letting me share our family life and for being patient in my mothering. To my own energetic and wonderful mother, my husband's dearly departed mother, and all mothers who do their best every day.

My heartfelt thanks to Cedar Fort Publishing for this

opportunity, and to my excellent editors Shersta Gatica and Kelley Konzak. And lastly to my fabulous critiquers—Rachael Anderson, Emily Cushing, Jill Holmes, Rhonda Miller, Quinn Silcox, and Judi Van Leeuwen—for making my writing shine.

Introduction

Trust in the Lord with all thine heart; and lean not unto thine own understanding.

Proverbs 3:5

The day after my husband and I took our oldest son to college (and our youngest had just entered first grade), I found out I was pregnant. With my seventh.

At age 45.

I wanted to gaze at the heavens and say, "Seriously?" Thoughts of scriptural heroines flashed through my mind, and though I did not laugh, I was sorely tempted to cry.

Our children felt understandably mixed at the news: one son stared in shock, a soon-to-be teenage daughter sobbed, and our college-aged son put it ever so succinctly when he said, "Are you guys crazy? Aren't six enough?"

Evidently not.

However, the irony was not lost on me. I had just signed a contract to write this Mother's Day gift book. I had agreed to start back on KSL's morning show *Studio 5* to be their motherhood contributor. I was asked by a magazine to write regular blog posts on—can you guess?—motherhood. And I was due, when else, in May—the month celebrating motherhood.

Was there a pattern here?

Beautifully, Heavenly Father did what He typically does—made things clear as I went along. In the initial research for this book, I read stacks of conference talks on diverse aspects of motherhood. As I pored through the pages, a profound gratitude spread through me for the gift and miracle of motherhood, as well as a yearning to keep that feeling in my soul continually. To remember that these same children who spread peanut butter on the new white couch are divine spirits sent in trust (in trust!) to you and me, everyday folk. Yes, we are divine too. But this deeper, more spiritually grounded vision of creating, raising, and mothering such divine children put the more immediate fears of dealing with sleep deprivation and potty training to rest.

And in perspective.

What follows here, then, is a book of joy—not a focus on to-dos or should-have-dones. It's simply a thank you, a congratulations, and an awe-inspired gratitude for all that women do as mothers.

This is the book to open when you've had it with mothering and want to run away to a nice hotel. Or when your children say you're fat. Or when the dryer breaks down, again.

This is the book to read when you want to be reminded of both the beauty and the majesty in motherhood. And this is definitely the book to read when, if nothing else, you want to laugh aloud at the most singular, magnificent, poignant, hilarious, heartbreaking, and transcendent experience a person can have in this life:

Motherhood.

THE
DIVINITY
OF MOTHERHOOD

Motherhood Is Divine

Motherhood is near to divinity. It is the highest, holiest service to be assumed by mankind," the 1942 First Presidency said.[1]

Despite what we see on a television screen or read in a magazine, motherhood is a holy calling and a divine privilege.

But how do we align the divine privilege of child-rearing with the reality of wiping green bean spit-up, or put cleaning the toilet in the context of "a holy calling"?

It is precisely because of the mundane and even distasteful that we come to see the holiness of what we do. "The Son of Man hath descended below them all. Art thou greater than he?" (D&C 122:8).

It's in the humble work and self-sacrifice that we find strength, honor, and valor to keep doing what needs to be done to forward something greater than ourselves—another divine human being.

Consider for a moment what you do daily to progress your children's lives, to help them learn the small lessons of life that build character and create a future thriving adult. These small but consistent acts are not insignificant—on the contrary. If you were not to teach them the ins and outs of daily life, who would?

President Spencer W. Kimball has said that despite what we may read, hear, or see as far as different circumstances in the women around us, it's important for us to remember that the Lord holds motherhood and mothers sacred and in the utmost respect.[2]

Motherhood is a divine calling, not an afterthought. Sister Sheri Dew shares that motherhood was not what was left over after Heavenly Father gave men the priesthood. It was and is the noblest endowment, a sacred trust, and an unequaled role in helping children keep this second estate. President J. Reuben Clark Jr. also declared that motherhood is as eternally and divinely important as the priesthood.[3]

Motherhood is beyond our scope in understanding the eternal ramifications of what we do. Years ago, General Relief Society President Barbara B. Smith told women to hold their heads high as homemakers because they engender and enrich life, and added, "You hold a mighty office."[4]

We do hold a mighty office. This isn't merely a feel-good platitude, it's an eternal truth. So today, in the midst of carpools and bake sales, remember the divine and timeless significance of your calling as a mother.

The Powerful Protection
of Motherhood

Elder Graham W. Doxey tells how his life was spared because of the prayer of his mother.

During World War II, he was in the navy and sent to China. One evening, after he and his fellow soldiers realized they were on a wrong train, they were let off in the countryside. Walking the train tracks, they found an old, small, pump-handle train car, which they would push uphill, then coast downhill.

On one steep hill slope, Graham was the last to get on, but he slipped and fell before securing a place. He bounced on his back on the track, with his feet against the car to keep it from running over him. At that moment, across the world, Graham's mother sat up at 2:00 in the morning and, waking her husband, said their son was in trouble. They knelt immediately in prayer for his safety.

Right then in China, Graham's sturdy military boot caught in a gear wheel and stopped the railroad car just one foot from cutting off his hand.

It was only after letters were exchanged, and both parents and son compared times, that they knew the miraculous and precise timing of the prayers on Graham's behalf.[1]

A mother's love can offer protection, even from across great distances. How often have we, or a mother we know, felt to pray, or call, or take action that has blessed a child's life?

"The effectual fervent prayer of a righteous [woman] availeth much" (James 5:16).

We don't often see dramatic results of our "effectual prayers" or deeds. But that doesn't make them any less needful or serviceable. When our oldest son went to college, I worried about the usual things—would he stay spiritually strong, eat right, get up for class, make good friends, and so on. Living a state away, I sometimes doubted my prayers or even care packages did that much for him.

But one day I received a priesthood blessing in relation to an illness that said, "Your prayers of faith will go a long way for [your son]. Be at peace concerning him." Immediately, I did feel peace, knowing that though it seemed so little, my prayers were both heard and purposeful in his behalf.

As righteous mothers we bless our families daily. We can rejoice in knowing we are able to call on the Lord at any time to protect those we love.

We Are All Mothers

Sheri Dew shares that Eve was called the "mother of all living" even before she had borne a single child. Although motherhood certainly includes bearing children, that is not all it involves. Motherhood is the very essence of who we are. Motherhood actually defines our identity, divine nature, and stature and is uniquely given to women alone.[1]

Whether single, married without children, or an empty nester with adult children, our physical situation in relation to children does not matter so much as that we love them. Mother Teresa bore no children of her own but mothered so fully that it became her title. Clara Barton, who never married, founded the Red Cross and was a "mother" to thousands of wounded soldiers.[2]

What matters is that we learn to love "mothering"—for it is a learning process—whether it be of our own children, our neighbors' children, or children we teach. In the process, we recognize with gratitude our womanly nature to nurture, and with humility, our partnership with Heavenly Father to participate in the magnificent power of creating and forging life.

Mothering gives us the opportunity to grow and become infinitely more than we could without it. We understand more about people, life, and our purpose here. We gain, as a result, a deeper eternal view and find greater strength and ability to carry on through difficult days.

Successful mothering is the very basis of a society's progression. President Spencer W. Kimball said that from history the important message comes that great women have cared more for their families than for themselves and that such women had an understanding of what truly matters in life.[3]

Whether as a mother of our own children or someone else's, "mothering" is a divine gift already within us. As we open and exercise that gift, not only are our lives fuller and richer, but also the lives of those we love.

A Spiritual Anchor in the Home

We are likely the first and most powerful spiritual examples for our children. Every righteous prayer, every patient fast, every page of scripture puts spiritual coins in our own and our family's bank accounts and helps create a spiritual anchor in the home.

Personal revelation is an individual spiritual gift that all worthy sisters can claim. Elder Bruce R. McConkie said that the life of Rebekah of the Old Testament was one of the greatest patterns in all the scriptures of what a woman can do to righteously influence her family.

"The children struggled together within her; and she said, If it be so, why am I thus? And she went to enquire of the Lord" (Genesis 25:22).

Elder McConkie says, "Now note it well. She did not say, 'Isaac, will you inquire of the Lord. You are the patriarch; you are the head of the house,' which he was. She went to inquire of the Lord, and she gained the answer."[1]

Rebekah didn't push it off on someone else but trusted in the Lord and found out for herself what the Lord desired her to do.

Repeatedly, scriptural heroines—Eve, Sarah, Esther, Ruth, and especially Mary, the mother of the Savior—show by example how to receive personal revelation and how it can bless our families. Scriptures show how these stalwart women knew doctrine and applied it in their lives, receiving inspiration, visitations, and miracles that changed not only their families' lives but also generations to come.

As mothers, we have more ready tools to increase that revelation than ever before. Spiritual basics such as prayer, easily accessible scriptures—both in print and online—Relief Society, visiting teaching, partaking of the sacrament, and monthly fasting all provide powerful ways to receive the Spirit.

Closer proximity to temples makes it more convenient to

attend frequently and with more opportunities to receive greater peace and timely answers.

Blogging with other mothers to share thoughts, ideas, and scriptural insights into mothering can create connection and invite spiritual solutions.

Though it is insignificant to the world, a spiritual foundation is a legacy we gain for ourselves and leave for our children through the eternities—helping them gain their own spiritual anchor and personal relationship with the Lord.

We Bear Children

Years ago my husband and I—pregnant with my third—traveled with our two young children to another state for a speaking assignment. I remember the obvious and incredulous stares we received upon entering restaurants and events. And that was only with two and a half children. Imagine the looks we received years later when we traveled with six!

President Spencer W. Kimball said that bearing children is women's irreplaceable work. Life in mortality is not only a privilege but also a necessary step in our progression.[1]

The world sees children as inconvenient, expensive, and an optional event—akin to buying a pet. Elder Neil L. Andersen shares a quote from a Christian mother not of our faith.

"Motherhood is not a hobby, it is a calling. You do not collect children because you find them cuter than stamps. It is not something to do if you can squeeze the time in. It is what God gave you time for."[2]

We know from scripture that "children are an heritage of the Lord" (Psalm 127:3). The purpose for everything we do and have—the Father's plan of happiness, the creation of the earth, all gospel principles, ordinances, and covenants—is to seal and exalt the family.

That being said, in all its divinity and wonder, the statement "we bear children" has a very real temporal side. Elder Andersen adds the story of a young mother entering a bus with seven children. The driver asked if the children all belonged to her or if they were going on a picnic. She responded that they were all hers, and it was no picnic![3]

It's vital to remember that the number of children we bear is not as significant as our desire to be a mother and what the Lord desires for our personal and family growth. Some women seem to easily conceive eight children while others spend years and expense trying to have one child. Sister Patricia Holland had three children but wept that she could not have more.[4] Every woman's situation is different.

But each moment we spend with our children—nurturing, teaching, loving—helps to create a future stellar adult who can help change the world, or at least change their own lives. We help them know how to walk the path back to their Father in Heaven, and we fulfill our vital honored stewardship in doing so.

No matter the media or society's influence, we can be grateful if we are able to bear children. Even amid the incredulous stares or non-picnic days, remember that you are doing something of eternal significance.

Mothers Are Incredible!

Historian Wallace Stegner observed something particularly noteworthy about the Mormon migration. He said, "Their women are incredible."[1]

Amen! If you ever doubt it, read the countless Church talks about your value and worth, and the grateful appreciation from leaders of the Church. President Spencer W. Kimball said that we had grown strong as an LDS people because the mothers and women had been so selfless.[2]

We are incredible! All that we do as women, wives, and mothers so often goes unnoticed and unappreciated, but it remains incredible nonetheless.

Elder Jeffrey R. Holland said of mothers, particularly young mothers, "The work of a mother is hard, too often unheralded work. . . . Through these years, mothers go longer on less sleep and give more to others with less personal renewal for themselves than any other group I know. . . . It is not surprising when the shadows under their eyes sometimes vaguely resemble the state of Rhode Island."[3]

I've been there. Often. And have looked forward to a future date when I would actually get a full night's rest. Then came teenagers. At last, I came to the conclusion that the underlying purpose of parenting is to ensure that we don't adequately sleep for the remainder of our mortal lives.

But we endure it anyway, knowing that this is part and parcel of the gift of being a parent and that without the investment, we wouldn't feel the love.

Know the appreciation of so many for each unsung act, unseen tear, and sleep-deprived night.

Mothers really are incredible.

THE
REALITY
OF MOTHERHOOD

There Is No Perfect Mother

Elder M. Russell Ballard has stated those very words.[1] Elder Larry R. Lawrence expanded it to say that "there are no perfect parents."[2] And when quiet, mothers can know for themselves, in their souls, that this is true.

There is no perfect way to "do" motherhood correctly. So we can give ourselves permission to be the best mother to *our* children without comparison to the seemingly perfect neighborhood mother (who does not exist).

One of my friends sent me the following email: "I will never be the 'culture perfect' mom but I'm the mom my children need. I buy crickets to feed the lizard. I rarely packed a lunch for them or made cookies, but they could make them since I showed them how, and let them do it whenever they were done with homework and felt like it."[3]

Some mothers sew their children's costumes—some buy them online with shopper savvy discounts. What matters is that we love and nurture and raise our children in the best ways *they* need it. That we deeply and fully love our children, apologize for mistakes, and do better tomorrow.

Lioness at the Gate

As a "lioness at the gate"—in the words of Sister Julie B. Beck—we are protectors and caregivers, watching over our children.[1]

This is not overbearing or hovering—it is proactive, involved, and aware. Whether it's positively monitoring our children's online activities, cell phones, and friendships, or tracking media in our homes, "lioness" moms are vigilant and determined.

Thankfully, the Lord will alert our instincts as we pay attention. One day while asking my son what he had been doing for the past hour, I noticed two things: he had been supposedly doing homework without a reminder, and he was unusually talkative and cheerful. Something was up. With that inner mother radar, I decided to check his cell phone. This led to a fabulous learning experience and a perfectly timed intervention to what could have been a not-so-great situation.

Elder D. Todd Christofferson paid tribute to his mother about the well-timed stop to his potential "life of crime" when, as a child, he stole a candy bar because of peer pressure from friends. Her diligent handling of the situation—having him earn and return the money—and instructive lesson on repentance stayed with him for many years.[2]

Small interventions make a tremendous future impact, and early awareness prevents a great deal of future misery. President Hinckley told how years ago, while working at a railroad, he received a call that a train had arrived without its baggage car. With some research, he discovered that a switchman had incorrectly moved the train switch about three inches. This made the train car go on the wrong track for 1,300 miles.[3]

Involved. Intuitive. Intervening. Mothers continually check the train switches to keep children on track. As we set the example, they can begin to check their own switches. That same son I mentioned above was also asked to a dance before he was sixteen years old. After discussion on *For the Strength of Youth* standards, and what as well as why the prophets have counseled no dating before sixteen, we asked him to pray about it. With wonderful maturity, he agreed to keep the standard and kindly let the girl know of his decision.

As lionesses, we watch and listen for any potential predator—inside or out—then swiftly act to keep our cubs safe and sound.

And though we do it kindly, we make no apologies. For these are our children and we know we are lionesses at the gate—a word of warning to those who approach!

Dirt under My Nails

S ister Marjorie Pay Hinckley shared a perfect quote that sums up real motherhood:

"I don't want to drive up to the pearly gates in a shiny sports car, wearing beautifully, tailored clothes, my hair expertly coiffed, and with long, perfectly manicured fingernails.

"I want to drive up in a station wagon that has mud on the wheels from taking kids to scout camp.

"I want to be there with a smudge of peanut butter on my shirt from making sandwiches for a sick neighbor's children.

"I want to be there with a little dirt under my fingernails from helping to weed someone's garden.

"I want to be there with children's sticky kisses on my cheeks and the tears of a friend on my shoulder.

"I want the Lord to know I was really here and that I really lived."[1]

This is living! Being in the thick of it is the core of motherhood. Of course, this doesn't mean we can't feel put together or wear trendy clothes, but it does mean that often we won't, despite our best intentions.

With consecutive pregnancies, taking children to activities, getting dinner on the table, and keeping up with family demands, life is first about being a mom and second about being hip. Designer jeans may be replaced with stretchy pants, or your business suit may be accessorized with peanut butter.

That's okay. Get in, get messy, and get those manicured nails dirty. President Thomas S. Monson said that if you're still raising young children, know that the messes children leave behind will disappear sooner than you think, and you'll find that you miss them.[2]

Don't worry about "the look." Yes, do your best and make your home a beautiful place, and present yourself in a lovely manner. But if it doesn't happen as often as you'd like, that's okay.

Just for today, put on a little lipstick and play hopscotch with your children—in your stretchy pants.

"She Had a Sunny Face"

In his landmark talk, "To the Mothers of Zion," President Ezra Taft Benson shared ten ways to be at the crossroads of our children's lives.

One particularly touching section was this tribute by a son to his mother: "She liked to lie on the grass with me and tell stories, or to run and hide with us children. She was always hugging me. . . . And I liked it. She had a sunny face. . . . Thinking of this, I wonder if the woman of today, with all her tremendous notions and plans, realizes . . . how much sheer love and attention count for in a child's life."[1]

Having a sunny face means we give so much to our children by the small and simple things.

Sister Beck said that when she was feeling down about all that needed improving as a mother, her daughter consoled her with the suggestion that she could at least smile.[2]

We can smile! We can have a sunny face. It doesn't need to be every minute of every day—and maybe not when a child has scraped down the side of the car with his bike handlebar—but in the thick of the daily thin of it, we can still, even for seconds, have a "sunny face."

Remember when they played in the mud the day you were trying to take family photos? Or when they took in a stray cat and it awoke the next day with kittens? Think on those moments that now make you smile and it can help you keep a "sunny face."

Consider the joys of motherhood at each stage of life—enjoying the sweet cuddles from freshly bathed children in their soft cotton pajamas. Celebrating with your teen that he aced that huge test. Helping your adult daughter with the birth of her first child.

These kinds of moments are motherhood magic that can give us a "sunny face."

Putting Motherhood First

In our day, opportunities for women to explore their personal potential are limitless. And we have been told that while focusing on motherhood, it is possible to fit other appropriate things into our lives.[1]

But from hobbies to business, the difficulty is not only staying focused on motherhood but also wisely choosing which extra activities fit our season. When presented with opportunities outside the core of motherhood, it may help to ask, "Will this bless my family or detract from it?"

Years ago I was a guest on a radio show. After the segment, the host turned to me and offered me my own show. At first it was tempting—a perfect way for me to get family concepts to a great number of people at one time. But at that point in life, I had a fairly new baby and other small children. Though it was only once a week, I knew from past experience there was a hidden cost of time, energy, and the unexpected. I turned it down.

A few years later I was approached again to host a radio show with a much larger radio station. This time the hours were the issue—full time, and in the afternoon when my children would be home. However, after prayer, I felt to negotiate the time frame and was able to receive an ideal situation that didn't conflict with my family.

Two similar situations but with different circumstances. Both had to be evaluated and prayed about before I could understand if they would have a positive or negative influence in my family's life.

Over the years, I've experienced this time and again with extra opportunities—from doing television and radio, to writing for magazines and newspapers, to a host of other "exciting" activities. In each case, I've had to delay, reduce, or forgo them to focus on motherhood first.

But amazingly, each opportunity has come back around, and in a way *better* suited for my life than the original.

Trust in the Lord. Trust His promises, "for he will fulfil all his promises which he shall make unto you" (Alma 37:17). He knows that fulfilling your role as a mother will bring you the greatest joy now and in the future, so trust in His wisdom to know what will keep it first.

The opportunity to be a mother to your children, at their particular stages, comes only once. Being there, being present, being an up-to-your-elbows part of their lives is our gift to receive. Daily connection bonds us to our children, gives them stability and confidence, and creates relationships where they will at some point "arise up, and call [us] blessed" (Proverbs 31:28).

Former reporter and author Maria Shriver shares a difficult experience in putting motherhood first. She and her production team were to interview the Cuban dictator Fidel Castro. Due to illness, it was decided in a meeting that the interview would be rescheduled for Monday. Worried, Maria burst out that she couldn't do it—she had to return home to take her daughter to her first day of school.

In the absolute silence that followed, her boss kicked her under the table and asked her to step outside. But despite an intense discussion, Maria remained firm.

Ultimately—and shockingly—Castro agreed that she should take her daughter to school and said that he would be ready for the interview the following Saturday.[2]

If Maria Shriver can stand down Cuban dictator Fidel Castro, we can surely stand up to a PTA member or a community service group that isn't helping us keep family first.

We get one time through with each child. Enjoy your present journey and know that truly great opportunities usually do come back, and often in a more appealing form.

Love Them When They're Unlovable

Part of divine parenting includes stressful day-to-day mothering. No matter how patient and loving a mother is, there will be those times in her life when *she has had it.*

President Harold B. Lee shares the experience of babysitting his grandson one night at a BYU football game. The little five-year-old began to be restless, and with merry looks from his fellow apostles, President Lee felt some pressure to have the evening go well.

After the boy fussed and was disobedient, President Lee tried to make him behave, but his grandson turned around and punched him in the face. President Lee wanted to take him out and spank him, as he felt that was what the boy deserved.

But then he remembered something his daughter would say: "You have to love your children when they're the least lovable."

So he took the boy in his arms and told him how much he loved him. His grandson's little body relaxed, and he kissed President Lee on the cheek. The boy had been conquered with love.[1]

That's what true mothering is: feeling one way—and justified in it—but choosing the higher path. Lehi and Sariah could have booted Laman and Lemuel out of the house—or overboard—and let them learn the hard lessons of life with a dose of angry retribution. And who would have blamed them? But their consistent, patient, and firm love made it possible for their wayward sons to have a clear choice in their behaviors, without anger getting in the way.

That doesn't mean as mothers that we don't set boundaries or give consequences. But it does mean that we think carefully about the emotion—or the approach—associated with it.

Love them when they're least lovable—that's what mothers do.

Lighten Up!

The story is told of a man driving on a precarious mountain road when a woman comes barreling around a corner, narrowly missing his car, and yells out the window, "Pig!" The man, incensed, yells back, "Sow, sow!" Then he turns the same corner and hits a pig.[1]

We get what we're looking for. So often we consume ourselves with the serious business of motherhood—*vital* things like the best-looking cupcakes at the class party—and end up losing the joy of the moment.

As mothers, we are doing so much better than we think or know (mainly because most people don't tell us and we are left to fear the worst).

One year my preschool daughter was given an assignment to bring a decorated poster to spotlight her as "Blossom of the Week." Excited, she and I planned to create it on a particular Sunday, a day that found me in a state of severe flu-like sickness.

By Tuesday, however, I was better, and had completely forgotten about said poster until about ten minutes before the carpool arrived. That was when my daughter said—with large Cindy Lou Who eyes filled with just as large tears—"Mommy, where's my poster?"

Oops.

Like a stadium fireworks display, I burst into action, grabbing glue, scrapbooking paper, stick-ons, and anything else that could spruce up the back of an old poster board. We worked feverishly, and as the doorbell rang, we finished the last stick-on.

Truly fearing the poster was hideous and that my daughter would become a preschool outcast, I asked my friend how the poster looked. She simply shrugged and smiled.

Devastation.

I spent the next fifteen minutes worried, anxious, and guilty that I had let my daughter down because of a lame, last-minute poster, and there went her star-like claim to "Blossom of the Week."

The phone rang. It was the preschool teacher. I knew it was about The Lame Poster—maybe I'd done it wrong. Perhaps it was supposed to include a biography. The first thing she said was, "That is the cutest poster I've ever seen."

Redemption!

It wasn't until later—an embarrassingly long period of time later—that I realized, what did it matter? If my daughter liked it, why should I worry about others' opinions?

The Blossom Poster experience taught me several key concepts, not the least of which was, to lighten up. It's a poster. It's a cupcake. It's a science fair project that a child is supposed to do, with *minimal* help.

Instead of each assignment, event, or life experience becoming monumental—and losing the joy between mother and child in the doing—we can bring the thing down to its core purpose and basic bottom line.

We can lighten up.

More Than a Meal

We know as mothers that food on the table is more than ingredients on a plate. What we do, every day, to create a family dinner is worthy of the highest praises because it's here, at the lowly kitchen table, that we connect.

President James E. Faust said that homemaking is primarily what you choose for it to be. Through the frustrations of it—frustrations that are part of life and are found in the work of fathers too—we can find satisfaction.[1]

Isn't that true? My husband runs hardwood floor installation crews. But I remember back in the day when he did everything himself, including the dreaded edging—down on his knees with a small sander, painstakingly going over every inch of floor edge.

I realized that his days were not unlike mine and that mundane backbreaking work is a part of life, no matter where it takes place.

Sister Julie B. Beck reminds us that nurturing is the same as homemaking, and it includes the daily tasks mothers face. Ultimately, women have the most influence in their homes.[2]

So remember that each day, we're not just doing tasks. We are not merely throwing in a load of wash or mopping the kitchen floor—yet again. We are showing love to those who matter most. And we are growing, nurturing, and creating an eternal family through our homemaking.

Faith in Our Children

Regardless of our children's choices, we can be assured of Heavenly Father's love for them, and for us.

President James E. Faust stated if we don't have problems with our children, we will if we simply wait long enough. Some children would challenge any parents, but at some point, they will feel the Lord's Spirit reaching after them and, whether in this life or the next, they will return.[1]

What matters most is that mothers feel comfort in this doctrine and continue to pray for difficult or wayward children, holding onto them with faith and trusting in the Lord's promises.

How comforting to know that prophets of all ages have struggled with their own children, all the way back to Adam with Eve and their son Cain. Even God the Father had a son who unwisely used his agency—"and we beheld, and lo, he is fallen! is fallen, even a son of the morning!" (D&C 76:27). And "the heavens wept over him" (D&C 76:26).

Difficult children are not a new concept, but it is often a rite of passage. Elder Lynn G. Robbins said, "A sweet and obedient child will enroll a father or mother only in Parenting 101. If you are blessed with a child who tests your patience to the nth degree, you will be enrolled in Parenting 505. Rather than wonder what you might have done wrong in the premortal life to be so deserving, you might consider the more challenging child a blessing and opportunity to become more godlike yourself . . . Could it be possible that you need this child as much as this child needs you?"[2]

We can take heart in knowing that as our children learn to properly use the principle of agency, they will make mistakes. It's part of the learning process. But as mothers, we can focus on being a spiritual beacon and a safe harbor that always welcomes them home.

Mother Moments

We all have them. In fact, I have often put "Loser" in front of that title to denote how those moments can make me feel.

Several years ago, my fifth-grade son called me from school about getting hit with the dodge ball at recess. This child had a history of calling about emergency situations such as having a sore finger or forgetting his favorite book. So I responded with my typical, "Are you bleeding? Vomiting? In severe pain?" To which he replied, "No." To which I then rejoined, "You're just building character."

A few days later, the same child called again with the same complaint, except adding that "it hurt really bad." I gave my spiel, he gave his spiel. I finished with a rousing, "You're building character."

A few days later, he called again. (Why do I keep answering, you may wonder.) This time he had smacked into a fence post while playing tag. We exchanged the usual questions with the usual answers, and I hung up feeling validated in staying firm but determined to turn down the ringer volume.

Thankfully, I didn't. The phone rang a few hours later, with someone telling me that my son had been "found on the bathroom floor throwing up." As I rushed into the school office, I saw him, pale as death, with a very possible concussion and the very nice office ladies staring at me in *that* way.

It was a Mother Moment.

When was your last mother moment? I say "last" because there will be many. One of my friends told me her son was honored at a huge banquet to celebrate athletes who had shown particular excellence. Wonderful, except that he didn't tell his mother. He came home from the well-attended event, handed her flowers and earrings provided for the mothers of the feted athletes, and said, "You were the only one that wasn't there."

How many times have we forgotten treats for the school picnic, missed a dance rehearsal, or, worst of all, left a child at an event? I feel great comfort in the passages from the New Testament:

"As they returned, the child Jesus tarried behind in Jerusalem; and Joseph and his mother knew not of it. . . . And when they found him not, they turned back again to Jerusalem, seeking him" (Luke 2:43, 45).

Can we feel a little bit better knowing that such divinely appointed parents as Mary and Joseph unknowingly left Jesus behind too?

But these Mother Moments are also instructive. They teach us of God's love and watchful care, despite our best efforts.

As a counselor in a Primary presidency, I attended a training in a distant city, carpooling with the other presidency members. I had confidently organized things at home and had even asked my son to come home early to be on time to babysit his five-year-old sister.

After the training, I called to see how the handoff went and immediately became alarmed. I had forgotten that this particular day was an "early-out," meaning my daughter had been home alone. And not only had she been alone, but in the ten minutes of aloneness, she had walked into the house, put a frying pan on the stove, and made scrambled eggs.

Did I mention she was five?

As I spoke to my daughter on the phone—"Mom, I did a life skill. I made eggs!" I praised her efforts and told her what a big girl she was. Then I hung up and bawled like a baby, with the presidency sitting in the car. Talk about loser mother—my five-year-old daughter could have burned herself, the house, or both!

But later, I realized (after much calming and chocolate-covered pretzels) that He watches over His children. That He constantly fills in the gaps. And though that doesn't mean bad things will never happen, we can know that, as mothers, if we do our best to live righteously, He will make up the difference.

When to Be at the Top of Your Game

Motherhood can be exhausting; there are no two ways about it. But beautifully, we often have greater control of our schedules than we believe.

As the mom, we get to set the boundaries and to say, this is enough. But only if we know when enough is enough!

Sister Julie B. Beck has said, "A good woman knows that she does not have enough time, energy, or opportunity to take care of all of the people or do all of the worthy things her heart yearns to do."[1]

Fabulously, you and I don't have to do it all. In fact, we are counseled *not* to do it all and not to "run faster or labor more than you have strength and means" (D&C 10:4).

Sister Beck encourages mothers to evaluate daily schedules and see the key times we need to be at the "top of our game"—so that when our best energy is needed, it's available.

For most women, it's the afternoon—that's homework and snack time, school lowdown, and daily chores. It's dinner prep and connection and getting children to after-school activities.

Without guilt, do what it takes to prepare for that shift. Rest fifteen minutes or allow a young child to watch an educational show while you cuddle with him quietly. Coordinate errands on one specific day. Postpone a personal house project and instead do it together for family home evening.

Perhaps our "top game" is at night when our children are finally willing to talk. Enlist your husband's help to put the other children to bed while you focus on the one. Or rotate each night with a different child for a fifteen-minute chat about anything.

Parenting takes time, energy, and planning. Feel good about cutting a few things out to make quality time available and make it count.

Elder Dallin H. Oaks has said that at times we need to give up some good things to do even better things that can help us increase our faith in the Savior and have stronger families.[2]

Our children won't likely express it, but we will feel the immediate benefits and long-term dividends of consciously making time to be at the "top of our game."

Creation Is Part of Who We Are

President Dieter F. Uchtdorf has said that creating is one of the strongest desires we have. No matter our different backgrounds and abilities, we all have a yearning to create.[1]

Creation is woven into our very being as women. As we acknowledge and appropriately tap into it, we bless not only ourselves but also others' lives.

And developing our talents can come in handy during times of need. The Prophet Joseph Smith's mother, Lucy Mack Smith, earned enough money painting oilcloth coverings that she was able to help provide food and furniture for her family.[2]

Cultivating our talents and abilities along the way makes us better women, wives, and mothers.

Stay interesting, have fun, keep yourself alive! Take a painting class, learn to cook Thai food, run that 5K race. This is all part of motherhood, and don't let anyone tell you different. Enjoy becoming—no need to make it a chore or put perfectionist parameters on it.

Create, live, share!

THE

REWARDS

OF MOTHERHOOD

The Highest Honor

Transcendent. Incalculable. We are told that the promised blessings of motherhood are almost beyond what we can imagine.[1]

President David O. McKay said, "The noblest calling in the world is motherhood. True motherhood is the most beautiful of all arts, the greatest of all professions. She who can paint a masterpiece, or who can write a book that will influence millions, deserves the admiration and plaudits of mankind; but she who rears successfully a family of healthy, beautiful sons and daughters, whose immortal souls will exert an influence throughout the ages long after paintings shall have faded, and books and statues shall have decayed or have been destroyed, deserves the highest honor that man can give, and the choicest blessings of God."[2]

Unlike a job or community service—as good as those are—motherhood creates a unique experience. Every day, our energies are spent directly on matters of eternity. Local causes may come and go, jobs may cease to exist, companies may close their doors. But as a mother, nothing we do is irrelevant.

We are not turning in a report—we are shaping a future god. We are not cleaning a city landmark—we are building a person's character, testimony, and life, affecting generations to come.

And What of Our 2,060?

When I think of the valiant mothers of Helaman's stripling warriors, I often see in my mind women from my neighborhood. Or dear friends. Or mothers of friends.

Mothers who tell their children no to certain video games and yes to certain activities. Mothers who drive carpools and make sure everyone uses a seat belt, who set curfews and check homework, who encourage healthy snacks and remind children to pray. Mothers who institute and uphold family rules, no matter how seemingly silly or insignificant.

We are the mothers of the warriors of tomorrow. And each time we hold fast to a principle or practice that blesses our family, we are strengthening their obedience and ability to survive what they will yet face.

Growing up, my family had strange rules. We were not allowed to say the word "pig" in a derogatory sense. Or "cow." Or other such potty farm words. I couldn't wear nylons until junior high, despite being the only cheerleader in knee socks. Regarding makeup, I was allowed *mascara* in ninth grade. And ear piercing had to wait until late junior high (it was so traumatic that I can't pinpoint the year).

Yes, those were socially bitter times. But as I look back—and even disagree (on the nylons definitely)—I'm grateful my mother set and stood by her rules of modesty and morality. I knew, regardless of a rule's specifics, that she loved and cared about what happened to me. And obeying the strange family rules kept me from situations that I didn't see until years later.

We can stay vigilant, even when receiving the rolling of the eyes, the heavy sigh, or the slamming of a bedroom door. Church leaders have counseled us that "parenting is not a popularity contest"[1] and to not be afraid to offend our children for righteousness.[2]

Good parents will likely have times of being downright hated by the fruit of their loins. Fear not. This too shall pass.

And as the stripling warriors could later say, "We do not doubt our mothers knew it" (Alma 56:48).

True to human nature, and this scripture, they will admit we were wise after the fact.

Our job as mothers is not to be popular, but to be principled. And to return the Father's children to Him, having been as faithful in parenting as possible.

The Influence of Good Mothers

All I am I owe to my mother. I attribute all my success in life to the moral, intellectual and physical education I received from her.

George Washington[1]

A true experience is told in *The Influencer* about the simple but miraculous solution to a life-threatening worm disease in Guinea, South Africa.

A research team was sent in to analyze the villages in the stricken areas, and they found one village was surprisingly disease-free. After observing this particular group's behaviors and patterns, the researchers discovered that when the women returned home from fetching water, they didn't use it right away.

Instead, they covered a second water container with their skirts and poured the water through the skirts into the pot.

Essentially, the skirts acted as strainers, eliminating the disease-causing larvae.

Because the women implemented that *one* small step they saved their village from a ravaging disease.[2]

That is a mother. By "small and simple things" (Alma 37:6), she is able to change the course of her family, a community, or a nation.

In our day, we have even greater influence than ever before. President Spencer W. Kimball has said that a righteous woman's influence in our day can be tenfold what it could have been in less turbulent times.[3] And that means our most important influence is spiritual, as we have been told that we are the spiritual glue that holds the family together.[4]

The stripling warriors didn't just say "Gee, our moms were really fun" or "Wow, our moms had a really clean tent." They said their mothers had taught them, first and foremost, what would anchor them to the divine. And it saved their lives, physically and spiritually.

That being said, spiritual is not our only influence. Every day, in a myriad of ways, our example shapes our children's responses: when we find money on an empty street and donate it to fast offerings; when we give up a coveted purchase to help a neighbor in need; when we put an arm around an unknown child who has fallen down.

Whether in dramatic or everyday experiences, we are influencing our children for good.

Rejoice in the Transitions

Our last goes to kindergarten, our first goes to college. Through tears and smiles, one thing stands true: transitions are constant in motherhood.

We can rejoice in them! We can celebrate having successfully raised and loved a child into the next stage in life, as we delight in their past milestones.

When my first child went to college, people repetitively asked if I was sad or doing okay. Are you kidding? I was thrilled! He is our son with Asperger's syndrome (high-functioning autism), and frankly, my husband and I were ecstatic that he had successfully come to this point in his life.

Of course we missed him, but that didn't make a dent in

the complete and utter joy we felt in his capacity to actually go to college, organize and live his daily life, and handle his own problems with wisdom and new experience.

As a parent, does it get any better than that?

So we can wipe our tears with the knowledge that we have done exactly what we set out to do—raise a future stellar adult, capable of living his or her own life and building on the lessons we have so carefully and lovingly taught.

"Wonderful," you may say. "But *now* what do I do?"

What can't you do? Take all that life learning and pour it into your other children or contribute to those around you.

A friend of mine felt a little lost when her last child went to school full-day. After a year of cooking classes and some self-care activities, she felt a lack of purpose. Then she went back to what she loved, and that tapped her potential—she started a preschool again.

This woman is incredibly talented at teaching children. What a blessing she now is to those young children who need her love as much as she needs theirs.

Use a transition to springboard yourself to greater growth.

My friend's son said to her—when all the children were back in school—"I guess this is when the whole stay-at-home mom thing starts paying off."

Absolutely! Don't feel guilty. You've got more time, so use it to create, serve, and live more fully.

President Spencer W. Kimball encouraged women to be absorbed with uplifting and enriching pursuits that could leave little time for negative, evil, or bored thoughts.[1]

We can allow Him to help us see all we have to offer. As we discover it, "line upon line, precept upon precept" (2 Nephi 28:30), we will feel the joy of contribution and keep feelings of self-pity at bay.

Now is the time to enjoy discovering what else we can contribute, not to the exclusion of motherhood, but in addition to it, and in our uniquely personal way.

Sacrifice Is Sanctifying

Elder Jeffrey R. Holland shares these lines attributed to Victor Hugo:

"She broke bread into two fragments and gave them to her children, who ate with eagerness.

"'She has kept none for herself,' grumbled the sergeant.

"'Because she is not hungry,' said a soldier.

"'No,' said the sergeant, 'because she is a mother.'"[1]

Sacrifice is an inherent part of motherhood. But before we leap to woe-is-me, think on how this one trait alone fits us for eternity.

"Verily I say unto you, all among them who know their hearts are honest, and are broken, and their spirits contrite, and are willing to observe their covenants by sacrifice . . . they are accepted of me" (D&C 97:8).

The Savior was perfect in every way, yet, until He had atoned for the sins of all mankind, He could not do all that He was to do or become. It was in the sacrifice that He learned the fulness of compassion, mercy, and love.

President J. Reuben Clark Jr. said, referring to faithful women of the scriptures and early Church history, that from then until now, the LDS woman has comforted the Church and borne more than half the burdens and sacrifices, and most of the heartaches.[2]

This is not a self-created sacrifice or a needless martyrdom of our lives. Real, required sacrifice is the kind that says, "I'd really rather not, if you don't mind. In fact, I don't want to do it at all. And if I could just add, *no thanks.*"

But then completing it with, "Nevertheless, thy will be done."

Years ago our oldest son was diagnosed with Asperger's syndrome. He struggled through several years of schooling. Intelligence was not an issue, but conforming to the rigid school day and its expectations was. At one point, I felt impressed to homeschool him. My first reaction was that neither of us would survive. And I meant it.

After a great deal of prayer—and fruitless bargaining with the Lord—the choice was clear to me. Not a voice or a command, but a simple choice: homeschool him or don't.

I wish I could say I was thrilled. I wasn't. Being with him at this time of his development was exhausting, and I had four other young children to care for. But to this day, I thank Him for helping me choose it. That experience, though it lasted only a few years, changed his and my life. And we reaped incredible fruits for many years. He went on to graduate from public high school with honors and to successfully attend Brigham Young University–Idaho.

What sacrifices have we made for our families? What blessings have we experienced as a result?

Sister Patricia Holland tells about her mother, who, while pregnant with Sister Holland, became ill and threatened to miscarry. The doctor said she was to stay down the entire pregnancy. For many months and without complaint, she lay on her back—literally in a tent, due to circumstances—while keeping two active boys entertained during the heat of summer and the cold of winter. Her neighbors told her to get up and lose the baby naturally, as it would likely be deformed anyway. But she didn't and was able to birth a lovely baby girl. Such valiant actions taught Sister Holland about the rewards of personal sacrifice.[3]

When the moment comes to sacrifice—big or small—we can look to others who have paved the path: Abraham taking Isaac to the mount, Sariah leaving her home and life in Jerusalem, Job losing all and still praising the Lord. No matter the type of sacrifice required—different in each of these situations—we know "that all these things shall give thee experience, and shall be for thy good" (D&C 122:7).

Joy in Motherhood

I t's all around us, present each day, and yet too many of us can't see or feel it—the tangible joy in motherhood.

We stand with our fixed faces and hands on hips and point and shoot interrogations—"Did you clean your bathroom? Did you do your homework? Did you take care of your chores?" Somewhere between barks, we can lose that lovin' feeling.

I was strongly reminded of the need for joyful awareness at my youngest daughter's dance class. A host of six-year-olds, giddy with newfound freedom, leapt, laughed, and ran all over the dance studio. The room felt fairly alive with their complete joy of movement. I turned to one of the mothers next to me and said, "*We* need this as moms."

The very next morning I attended my Zumba exercise class, where women do enjoy the fun but, let's face it, are motivated by the calorie-burning benefits. That time our instructor had us do a particular Latin dance where we gathered in a circle and started in slow movements, then got faster and faster until we were moving lightning fast in the circle.

Laughing and throwing our arms in and out with energetic abandon, we then held hands and gathered in the center, at which time I hollered, "Opa!" Our shift in attitude and energy was incredible!

That's the gems of everyday joy we can find and feel: make a special cake for when the kids come home, just because. Forgo ego—and calorie-burn—and allow our children to beat us in a Wii bowling tournament (which, frankly, is not that hard). Read with one child, cuddling on her bed for special time together. Enjoy the unexpected joke, the stunning sunset, the newly discovered giant moth on the front porch.

These are the moments not to be missed but to be tasted and savored, felt and remembered.

Women at the
Washing Well

As mothers, we women need each other, often more than we did as singles.

Because motherhood can be a lonely job. It's home-centered, and at some stages that means practically duct-taped to the walls. But realizing our need to be with, learn from, and extend ourselves to other women, we can create synergistic connections. We can feel uplifted, energized, and ready to boldly go where no mother has gone before.

"They . . . shall renew their strength; they shall mount up with wings as eagles; they shall run, and not be weary; and they shall walk, and not faint" (Isaiah 40:31).

Friendship is the leaven that makes the loaf of motherhood

rise again and again. It gives encouragement and validation where we find only fatigue. It motivates and inspires where we see only the daily grind of repeat routines. It is the sparkle and zest that provides energy and renewed determination when we feel we can't go on.

Consider the love and service that we've received from close friends. Rejoice in the goodness of good women and all they teach and bring. Celebrate that we are those women and how many—how very many—we have lifted along the way.

To deepen our friendships we can open ourselves to the *opportunity* of connection, if only for a few moments.

Keep in touch with other women daily if possible—stop at the mailbox and say hello. Pause in the grocery store aisle and ask how someone's doing. Take a moment here and there, and you'll be surprised at how full your bucket inadvertently becomes.

Nothing Is Wasted

Many women come from an active and accomplished single life and walk through the new and mysterious portals of motherhood only to find that their biggest accomplishment is finding a matched pair of socks before the bus comes.

Some days we can think, "Is this what I got a degree for?" But we forget that child-rearing is a grand and ongoing experience and that what we bring to motherhood matters. Everything we've learned, and are, and have become, is now transferred in countless ways to our children.

Sister Julie B. Beck shares that her mother married when she was older. Surprising for the times, her mother had become university-educated and progressed in a career. But after marriage—and a quick succession of children—she channeled all her developed gifts and abilities into motherhood. In this way, she had literally prepared all her life for her calling.[1]

In my own life, I've used pre-motherhood abilities such as my elementary education degree, writing, typing, singing, organizing, the creative arts, and my travel experiences, to name a very few.

One of my favorites has been using my theater skills from acting in plays during college. It's come in handy. One of our sons went through a period of lying about low grades—not all the time, but enough that it was frustrating and disheartening. We tried a variety of methods to help him change his behavior, but to no avail.

Finally, one day after receiving an email from a teacher that told me of his failing academic status—when the day before our son had claimed A grades—I'd had enough.

After talking with my husband, I waited until our son came home and said, "Dad and I were talking about how fabulously you've done with your grades. Because you've been so good and diligent, we're getting you a yearlong snowboarding pass *and* a pass for one of your friends." His eyes widened to the size of giant olives. I continued. "And, seeing as your grades are *so* good, we thought we'd celebrate with a big pizza party with all your friends."

He was taken aback and he was thrilled, but with a hint of guilt behind the eyes. He said, "Really? That's great!" With a straight face, I said, "Isn't it? Because it's a lie. Just like you lied to us about your grades. And now you know how it feels."

That was the last time he lied about his grades.

In motherhood, every single talent and ability, each bit of wisdom and knowledge not only aren't wasted, but also continually come into play.

Remember that life is a continuum. We can return to that degree, we can pick up that old hobby again, all within the time frame of motherhood as it works best for our family. But in the meantime, what we gain by everyday study, delight, or practice is immediately used in raising our children.

No part of us that came before children is ever, ever wasted, nor what we create as we go along.

Share liberally.

My Piece of Foreign Sky

You are the trip I did not take;
You are the pearls I cannot buy;
You are my blue Italian lake;
You are my piece of foreign sky.[1]

Motherhood means giving up some things—important things, things that are personally meaningful to us as women—and usually at the most pivotal or inconvenient times.

To celebrate our fifteenth wedding anniversary, my husband and I planned a trip with friends to Italy. Going to that beautiful country had been my lifelong dream, and for many years I had posted the goal and pictures of cities in Italy on a board in my room. I had even taken a year of Italian in college.

However, months before the trip, I felt in my soul that my

younger children were too young for me to leave them for an extended time, and I chose not to go.

That was hard.

However, I wouldn't trade that time with my children or change my decision. And though that personal goal has not changed—I still post pictures of Italy on a board in my room—it will happen at the best time for my family.

Perhaps we've sacrificed a promising career or education. Maybe our health has suffered or we've lived in the same old house to be "fixed up" at some future point. It could be that our foreign sky is not foreign at all—it's just trying to get to an aerobics class, but we can't because we have little ones.

Throughout the stages of motherhood, there are those feelings of denial—from small things, such as what we'd really like for lunch (when the reality is peanut butter and jelly—again), and the bigger things, such as writing a novel or finishing college.

But we can adjust.

One woman I know took twenty years to finish her college degree—yet she did it. One or two classes per year, bit by bit, keeping at it until she had her degree in hand.

We can rejoice in our children *and* keep planning for that trip we cannot take and that piece of foreign sky.

It will be ours. And with our family to rejoice in it together.

Hold Your Soul Very Still

Relish time spent quietly, without feeling guilty or considering something more productive.

President James E. Faust says to *hold our souls very still* and listen to the whisperings of the Holy Spirit—to continue to follow the noble, intuitive feelings planted within our souls.[1]

Linda J. Eyre, author and mother of nine, states that, as mothers, we need to be "selfish" enough at least once a week to spend time alone.[2] Sister Eyre takes an hour to herself each Sunday night—to plan, think, and be still. This gives her not only a clear schedule but also vital rejuvenation.

Consider ways you can be still, then relish the time without guilt or worry. Opening our souls to that peaceful, insightful voice gives us access to greater energy and spiritual insights. "Be still, and know that I am God" (Psalm 46:10).

Be Yourself

I love this quote from Leo Buscaglia on Julia Child: "I watch her because she does such wonderful things: 'Tonight, we're going to make a soufflé.' And she beats this and she whisks that, and she throws things on the floor. She wipes her face in her napkin and she does all these wonderful human things. . . . And when she opens [the oven up, the soufflé] caves in. . . . She says, "Well, you can't win 'em all. Bon apetite!'"[1]

Be your wonderfully human self! Locked the keys in the car? Oh well. Sent Johnny to school in already-worn jeans because you forgot to do wash? There you are. You and I can stop taking ourselves so seriously and enjoy the humanness that makes us real people.

One morning, as the host of a radio show, I walked into the large professional office, meeting and greeting several people, when I looked down and saw that I was wearing two different shoes. Having been unable to decide which to wear, I'd forgotten to change one of them out!

Laughing hysterically, I went right on the air and shared my experience, to which many women responded they'd had not only the same experience, but even funnier ones. Oh well!

President Dieter F. Uchtdorf says, "To me it appears that our splendid sisters sometimes undervalue their abilities—they focus on what is lacking or imperfect rather than what has been accomplished and who they really are."[2]

So feel the joy in our humanness and share it with others. Don't focus on what seems imperfect, but rather, on who we really are.

A Thousand Brushstrokes

How many dishes have we done, dinners have we made, and homework assignments have we assisted with? How many family home evenings have we made sure were held, or scripture study sessions (what we often call "attempts"), or family prayers?

Day after day, week after week, year after year, each choice, action, and service is creating the most beautiful, powerful, and life-changing scene we can imagine for our family.

That's because every single good thing we do is a brushstroke that counts—nothing is overlooked or unused. Whether now or in the eternities, we will see the collective handiwork of the many strokes we have painted as a mother, and the result will be priceless.

Elder David A. Bednar said that at times, he and his wife wondered if their spiritual parenting efforts were worthwhile. Scripture study would be interrupted with "He's touching me" or "Make him stop looking at me." However, he says that today their adult sons wouldn't remember those things. What they would likely remember is that they were consistent.

Elder Bednar shares the beautiful analogy that each family prayer, scripture study, and family home evening is "a brush-stroke on the canvas of our souls."[1]

Mothers are phenomenal at daily doing what will ultimately yield the best and most long-lasting results. Know that every carpool, ride to the Young Women activity, or late night waiting up for a child is a blessing to both us and our families.

"Wherefore, be not weary in well-doing, for ye are laying the foundation of a great work. And out of small things proceedeth that which is great" (D&C 64:33).

Help of the Angels

M others are not alone in their holy, often overwhelming calling.

President James E. Faust affirmed his belief that angels attend mothers in their motherly ministry.[1]

Elder Jeffrey R. Holland testified that angels are still sent to help us, even as they were sent to prophets of old, and even to the Savior of the World.[2]

And Elder Bruce C. Hafen said that angels come when we seek to be worthy and we need them most.[3]

We can feel the help of heaven if we listen and look and prepare for it.

One member of the Martin handcart company said, "I have

pulled my handcart when I was so weak and weary from illness and lack of food that I could hardly put one foot ahead of the other. . . . I have gone on [to some point I thought I could never get past only to feel that] the cart began pushing me. *I have looked back many times to see who was pushing my cart, but my eyes saw no one. I knew then that the angels of God were there.*"[4]

We are not alone. These are His children. And He knows best what they need and how we can help. Ask. Listen. Follow and know that He trusts you and I to do the right thing. And when it feels overwhelming, exhausting, or too hard to keep going, remember that He will send help.

"Have angels ceased to appear unto the children of men? Or has he withheld the power of the Holy Ghost from them? Or will he, so long as time shall last, or the earth shall stand, or there shall be one man upon the face thereof to be saved?

"Behold I say unto you, Nay; for it is by faith that miracles are wrought; and it is by faith that angels appear and minister unto men" (Moroni 7:36–37).

References

The Divinity of Motherhood

Motherhood Is Divine

1. David O. McKay, Conference Report, Oct. 1942, 12–13.
2. Spencer W. Kimball, "Privileges and Responsibilities of Women," *Ensign*, Nov. 1978, 101.
3. Sheri L. Dew, "Are We Not All Mothers?," *Ensign*, Nov. 2001, 96.
4. *Daughters in My Kingdom: The History and Work of Relief Society* (Salt Lake City: The Church of Jesus Christ of Latter-day Saints, 2011), 158.

The Powerful Protection of Motherhood

1. Boyd K. Packer, "Prayers and Promptings," *Ensign*, Nov. 2009, 43–49.

We Are All Mothers

1. Dew, "Are We Not All Mothers?," 96.

2. Wikipedia, sv "Clara Barton" http://en.wikipedia.org/wiki/Clara _Barton.

3. Kimball, "Privileges and Responsibilities of Sisters," 101.

A Spiritual Anchor in the Home

1. Bruce R. McConkie, "Our Sisters from the Beginning," *Ensign*, Jan. 1979, 61–63.

We Bear Children

1. Kimball, "Privileges and Responsibilities of Sisters," *Ensign*, Nov. 1978.

2. Neil L. Andersen, "Children," *Ensign*, Nov. 2011.

3. Ibid.

4. Patricia T. Holland, "One Thing Needful: Becoming Women of Greater Faith in Christ," *Ensign*, Oct. 1987, 26.

Mothers Are Incredible!

1. Quentin L. Cook, "LDS Women Are Incredible!," *Ensign*, May 2011.

2. Kimball, "Privileges and Responsibilities of Sisters," 101.

3. Jeffrey R. Holland, "Because She Is a Mother," *Ensign*, May 1997, 35.

The Reality of Motherhood

There Is No Perfect Mother

1. M. Russell Ballard, "Mothers and Daughters," *Ensign*, May 2010, 18–21.

2. Larry R. Lawrence, "Courageous Parenting," *Ensign*, Nov. 2010, 98–100.

3. Author has email on file.

Lioness at the Gate

1. Julie B. Beck, BYU Women's Conference, opening session, 29 April 2010.

2. D. Todd Christofferson, "Moral Discipline," *Ensign*, Nov. 2009, 105–8.

3. Gordon B. Hinckley, "Watch the Switches in Your Life," *Ensign*, Jan. 1973, 91.

Dirt Under My Nails

1. "Marjorie Pay Hinckley Quotes," www.goodreads.com/author/quotes /226482.Marjorie_Pay_Hinckley.

2. Thomas S. Monson, "Finding Joy in the Journey," *Ensign*, Nov. 2008, 84–87.

"She Had a Sunny Face"

1. "To the Mothers of Zion," address by President Ezra Taft Benson at a fireside for parents on 22 February 1987.

2. Julie B. Beck, BYU Women's Conference, opening session, 29 April 2010.

Putting Motherhood First

1. James E. Faust, "How Near to the Angels," *Ensign*, May 1998, 95.

2. Maria Shriver, *Ten Things I Wish I'd Known Before I Went Out into the Real World* (New York: Warner Books, 2000), 80–81.

Love Them When They're Unlovable

1. Harold B. Lee, "Love at Home," chap. 14 in *Teachings of Presidents of the Church: Harold B. Lee* (Salt Lake City: The Church of Jesus Christ of Latter-day Saints, 2000), 129.

Lighten Up!

1. Leo F. Buscaglia, *Living, Loving & Learning* (New York: Fawcett Columbine, 1983), 214.

More than a Meal

1. Faust, "How Near to the Angels," 95.
2. Julie B. Beck, "Mothers Who Know," *Ensign*, Nov. 2007, 76–78.

Faith in Our Children

1. James E. Faust, "Dear Are the Sheep That Have Wandered," *Ensign*, May 2003, 61.
2. Lynn G. Robbins, "What Manner of Men and Women Ought Ye to Be?," *Ensign*, May 2011, 103–5.

When to Be at the Top of Your Game

1. Julie B. Beck, "And upon the Handmaids in Those Days Will I Pour Out My Spirit," *Ensign*, May 2010, 10–12.

2. Dallin H. Oaks, "Good, Better, Best," *Ensign*, Nov. 2007, 104–8.

Creation Is Part of Who We Are

1. Dieter F. Uchtdorf, "Happiness, Your Heritage," *Ensign*, Nov. 2008, 117–20.
2. Jaynann Payne, "Lucy Mack Smith: Woman of Great Faith," *Ensign*, Nov. 1972, 68.

The Rewards of Motherhood

The Highest Honor

1. Joanne B. Doxey, "Strengthening the Family," *Ensign*, Nov. 1987, 90.
2. David O. McKay, "The Noble Calling of Parents," chap. 16 in *Teachings of Presidents of the Church: David O. McKay* (Salt Lake City: The Church of Jesus Christ of Latter-day Saints, 2003), 152–61.

And What of Our 2,060?

1. Joe J. Christensen, quoted in Larry R. Lawrence. "Courageous Parenting." *Ensign*, Nov. 2010.
2. Robert D. Hales, in Lawrence, "Courageous Parenting."

The Influence of Good Mothers

1. George Washington, "Quotes," http://www.mothers.net/mothersquotes2.htm.

2. Kerry Patterson, Joseph Grenny, et al., *The Influencer* (New York: McGraw-Hill, 2008), 36.

3. *Daughters in My Kingdom*, 165.

4. M. Russell Ballard, "Women of Righteousness," *Ensign*, Apr. 2002, 66–73.

Rejoice in the Transitions

1. Kimball, "Privileges and Responsibilities of Sisters," 101.

Sacrifice Is Sanctifying

1. Holland, "Because She Is a Mother," 35.

2. J. Reuben Clark, Conference Report, Apr. 1940, 21.

3. Jeffrey R. Holland and Patricia T. Holland, *On Earth as It Is in Heaven* (Salt Lake City: Deseret Book, 1989), 18–19.

Nothing Is Wasted

1. Julie B. Beck, "A Mother Heart," *Ensign*, May 2004, 75.

My Piece of Foreign Sky

1. Anne Campbell, "To My Child," quoted in Charles L. Wallis, ed., *The Treasure Chest* (Harper & Row, 1965), 54.

Hold Your Soul Very Still

1. Faust, "How Near to the Angels," 95.

2. Linda Eyre, *A Joyful Mother of Children* (Salt Lake City: Shadow Mountain, 2000), 196.

Be Yourself

1. Buscaglia, *Living, Loving & Learning*, 260.
2. Uchtdorf, "Happiness, Your Heritage," 117–20.

A Thousand Brushstrokes

1. David A. Bednar, "More Diligent and Concerned at Home," *Ensign*, Nov. 2009, 17–20.

Help of the Angels

1. James E. Faust, "The Highest Place of Honor," *Ensign*, May 1988, 36.
2. Jeffrey R. Holland, "The Ministry of Angels," *Ensign*, Nov. 2008, 29–31.
3. Bruce C. Hafen, "When Do the Angels Come?," *Ensign*, Apr. 1992, 12.
4. James E. Faust, "The Refiner's Fire," *Ensign*, May 1979, 53. Emphasis added.